Iam books

Published by
I am Books
327-32 1116ho, Daeroung Techno Town 12cha
Gasan-dong, Kumcheon-gu, Seoul, Korea 153-802
TEL 82-2-6343-0999
FAX 82-2-6343-0995~6
www.iambooks.co.kr

Publisher Sangwook Oh, Sunghyun Shin
Author TIMES CORE The Junior Times
Editor Sungwon Lee, Dahhyun Gang, Jinhee Lee
Design Mijung Oh, Ran Park
Illustrations Soyoung Cho
Marketing Shindong Jang, Shinkuk Jo, Jinhee Jung, Misun Jang

ISBN 978-89-6398-056-0 64740

Yellow
Book
2

JUNIOR READING Start

How to Study This Book

01 Before reading articles, listen to audio files carefully two or three times.

02 Underline words that you are not familiar with, reading aloud the article.

03 Read the article one more time, making a guess the meaning of words.

04 Look up the dictionary to find out the meaning of words.

05 Memorize words that you don't know and try to solve the word tip quiz.

06 Read the article once again and answer the questions.

07 Lastly, listen to the audio file one more time focusing on the words you've learned.

CONTENTS

unit 01 What is the smallest bird in the world? 06

unit 02 Nelson Mandela became 93 years old 10

unit 03 Brazil elected first woman president 14

unit 04 Who has the longest tongue in the world? 18

unit 05 Go outside to be healthy! 22

unit 06 The youngest Everest climber 26

unit 07 The smallest monkey in the world 30

unit 08 Play safely in the playground! 34

unit 09 Remembering Kim Dae-joong 38

unit 10 I have the longest mustache in America 42

unit 11 The most popular soccer player in the world 46

unit 12 How do I look in the portrait? 50

unit 13 Do zebras lie down when they sleep? 54

unit 14 Walking safety 58

unit 15 Take care of your ears! 62

ANSWERS 66

UNIT 01

What Is the Smallest Bird in the World?

There are many kinds of birds in the world. But what is the smallest bird in the world? I'll give you some hints; it weighs only about 1.8 grams. It is about 5 centimeters tall. The tiny bird lives in Cuba. It flaps its wings 80 times per second! It can also fly backwards. Can you guess the name of the bird? It's the Bee Hummingbird!

Staff reporter Samuel Sohn

Writing

Let's look at the picture. Fill in the blanks and complete the sentences.

① bird ② lives ③ smallest ④ tall ⑤ weighs

(a) What is the ( ) bird in the world?

(b) The ( ) is the Bee Hummingbird.

(c) The bird ( ) only about 1.8 grams.

(d) The bird is about 5 centimeters ( ).

(e) The tiny bird ( ) in Cuba.

Word Tip

kind ______	the smallest ______	hint ______	weigh ______
tiny ______	live in ______	flap ______	날개 ______
(몇)번 ______	1초당 ______	뒤로 ______	추측하다, 생각하다 ______
꿀벌새 ______			

Grammar

Circle the right word to complete each sentence.

(a) Have you ever [**seen** / **see** / **saw**] the smallest bird in the world?

(b) There are [**much** / **more** / **many**] kinds of birds in the world.

(c) The tiny bird flaps its wings 80 [**times** / **time** / **timing**] per second!

(d) The Bee Hummingbird can [**fly** / **flew** / **flying**] backwards.

(e) Can you guess the name [**from** / **of** / **at**] the bird?

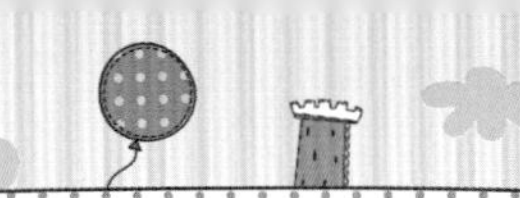

03 Question Vocabulary

Find the words used in the story in the puzzle below.

M	A	G	L	W	S	W	B	R	O
G	D	O	Q	A	V	H	I	N	T
W	J	G	B	S	G	G	R	C	E
L	E	G	C	H	E	M	D	S	T
H	T	I	N	Y	U	E	L	T	M
J	V	Y	G	E	F	R	F	A	N
S	T	Y	K	H	H	G	I	R	W
P	O	A	C	R	L	W	Q	I	E
P	B	A	O	W	Y	H	N	I	B
Q	E	X	P	E	N	G	I	V	E

Words

WEIGH / TINY / BIRD / HINT / WING

Nelson Mandela Became 93 Years Old

On July 18, 2011, Nelson Mandela celebrated his 93rd birthday with his family. He was born on July 18, 1918, in South Africa. He was the President of South Africa from 1994 to 1999. He was a great leader. Many people all over the world still respect him. Stay healthy, Mr. Mandela!

Staff reporter Daniel Chang

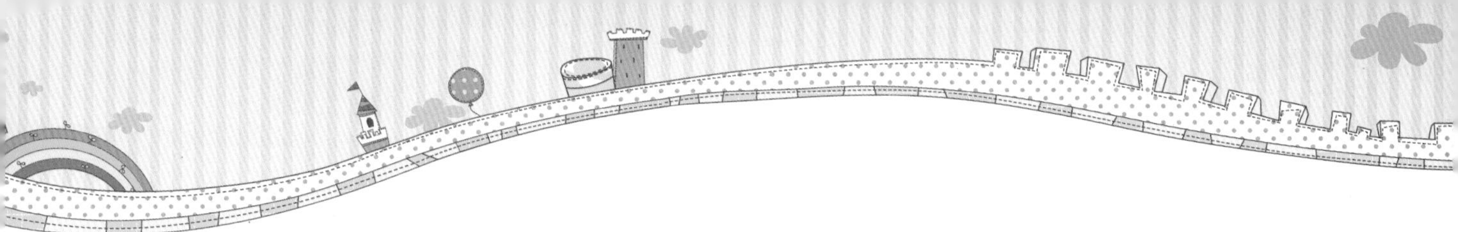

Writing I

Use the words below when you make the sentences.

celebrate / still / President / former / respect
Nelson Mandela / birthday / South Africa

(a) Who is the man with grey hair sitting on the sofa?

→ He is ____.

(b) What are they doing?

→ They are ____.

(c) How do the people all over the world think of him?

→ People all over the world ___________________________.

Word Tip

celebrate ________	be born ________	President ________	지도자 ________
존경하다 ________	건강하게 지내다 ________		

Grammar

Circle the right word to make the sentence correct.

(a) [**In** / **On** / **At**] July 18, 2011, Nelson Mandela celebrated his 93rd birthday with his family.

(b) He [**born** / **was born** / **were born**] on July 18, 1918 in South Africa.

(c) He was the President of South Africa [**from** / **between** / **among**] 1994 to 1999.

(d) Many people all over the world [**never** / **already** / **still**] respect him.

Writing II

Write your own story describing the picture below.

Hint: Be creative!

What is she doing?

____

____

____

____

____

____

____

____

____

04 Question Vocabulary

Let's finish the cross word puzzle below related to the story.

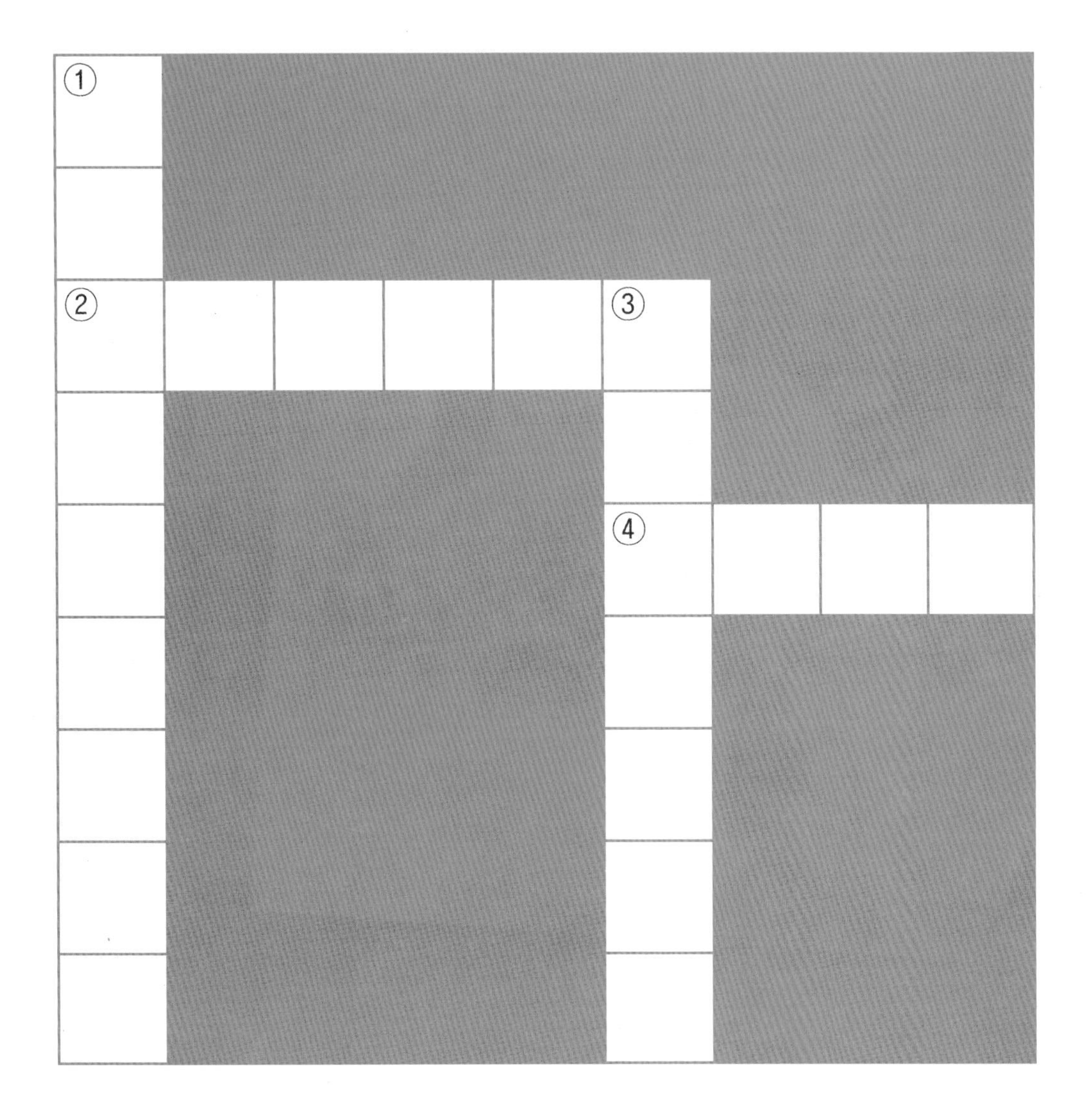

Across

② The person who is in control of a group or a country

④ To be there without leaving

Down

① To take part in special enjoyable event

③ To admire someone who is great

UNIT 03

BRAZIL

Brazil Elected First Woman President

On October 31, 2010, Dilma Rousseff became the first female president of Brazil. She said she was very happy to become her country's first female leader. She promised to work hard for her country. She started working as the president from January 1, 2011. Congratulations, Ms. Rousseff! Please make Brazil a better country!

Staff reporter Erica Choi

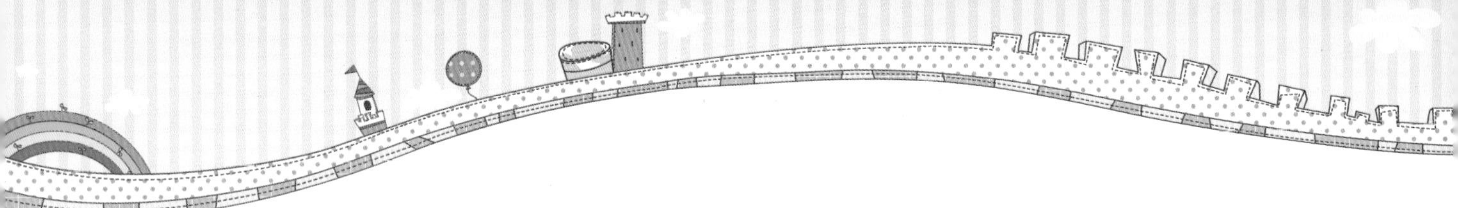

Comprehension

Read each question and find the right answer.

(a) What is the main topic of the article?

① Brazil is a South American country.
② The first woman president was elected in Brazil.
③ Ms. Rousseff said she was happy.
④ There were many female leaders in Brazil.

(b) Write down three words that begin with 'F' in the article.

① ____________________

② ____________________

③ ____________________

(c) When did she start working as the president?

____ .

Word Tip

become ________	female ________	leader ________	promise ________
~를 위해 열심히 일하다 ________	~로서 일하다 ________	더 나은 ________	

02 Question Vocabulary

Choose the right word to complete each sentence.

(a) On October 31, 2010, Dilma Rousseff became the first (   ) president of Brazil.

① famous
② fair
③ female
④ free

(b) She said she was very happy to become her country's first female (   ).

① athlete
② teacher
③ father
④ leader

(c) She (   ) to work hard for her country.

① promised
② proposed
③ practiced
④ picked

Comprehension

Look at the picture below and then answer the questions.

(a) Who is she?

① She is the first female singer in Brazil.
② She is the first female leader in Bosnia.
③ She is the first female teacher in Brazil.
④ She is the first female president of Brazil.

(b) What does she do?

① She sings cheerful songs for people.
② She leads the Brazilian people.
③ She works for the president in Brazil.
④ She works at the most famous restaurant in Brazil.

(c) What did she promise?

① She promised to help the poor.
② She promised to run for president.
③ She promised to work hard for her country.
④ She promised to donate a lot of money.

UNIT 04

Who Has the Longest Tongue in the World?

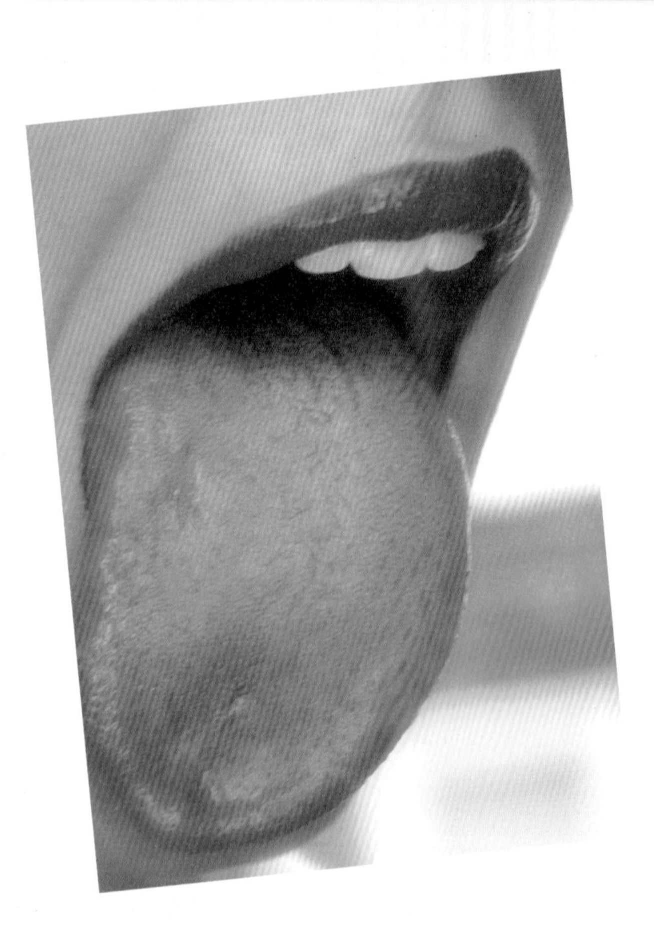

Do you know who has the world's longest tongue? According to the Guinness Book of World Records, a man who lives in the UK has the longest tongue in the world. His name is Stephen Taylor. So, how long is his tongue? Don't be surprised; It is 9.5 centimeters long! Wow! That's really long!

Staff reporter Samuel Sohn

01 Question Writing

Let's look at the picture. Fill in the blanks and complete the sentences.

① lives ② who ③ long ④ longest ⑤ name

(a) Do you know (   ) has the world's longest tongue?

(b) The man has the (   ) tongue in the world.

(c) The man (   ) in the UK.

(d) His (   ) is Stephen Taylor.

(e) His tongue is 9.5 centimeters (   ).

Word Tip

longest	tongue	~에 따르면	~에 살다
______	______	______	______
놀라다			
______			

Grammar

Circle the right answer to complete each sentence.

(a) Don't be surprised [**at** / **from** / **by**] the news!

(b) [**Who** / **Whom** / **Which**] has the longest tongue in the world?

(c) According [**at** / **for** / **to**] the Guinness Book of World Records, a man lives in the UK has the longest tongue in the world.

(d) Stephen Taylor [**has** / **have** / **is**] the longest tongue in the world.

(e) How [**far** / **long** / **much**] is his tongue?

Vocabulary

Find the words used in the story in the puzzle below.

M	A	G	L	Z	X	W	D	R	O
G	D	O	Q	D	C	E	A	V	I
B	N	O	T	Y	G	C	F	C	E
G	J	G	F	E	F	U	P	S	M
C	T	O	N	G	U	E	I	K	A
V	V	Y	U	E	F	R	F	J	N
O	I	C	K	I	P	O	W	Z	A
I	U	A	C	R	L	W	Q	H	E
P	R	A	U	I	P	Y	T	G	F
Q	X	S	T	B	W	O	R	L	D

Words

WORLD / LONG / TONGUE / SURPRISE / NAME

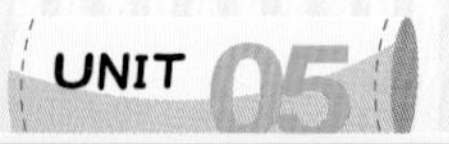

Go Outside to Be Healthy!

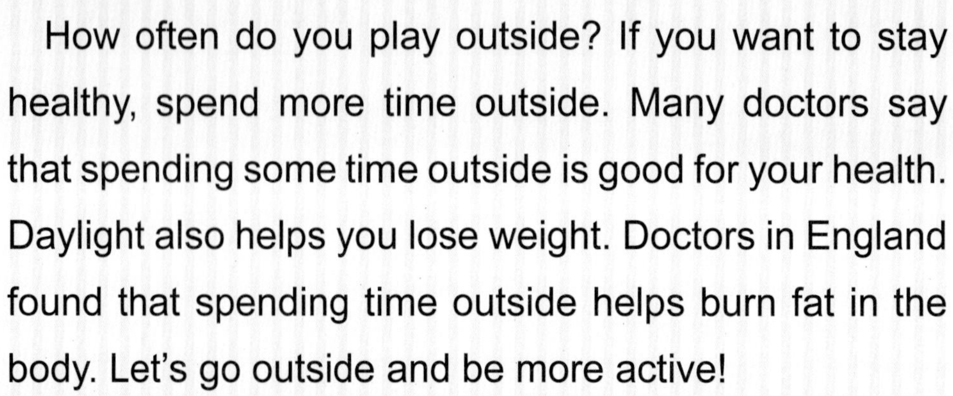

How often do you play outside? If you want to stay healthy, spend more time outside. Many doctors say that spending some time outside is good for your health. Daylight also helps you lose weight. Doctors in England found that spending time outside helps burn fat in the body. Let's go outside and be more active!

Staff reporter Daniel Chang

Comprehension

Let's look at the picture and fill in the blanks.

Hint: Answers are in the article.

Two girls in the picture are roller skating.

(a) If you want to stay h _ _ _ _ _ _, s _ _ _ _ more time outside.

(b) Daylight also helps you lose w _ _ _ _ _.

(c) Spending time outside helps b _ _ _ fat in the body.

(d) Let's go outside and be more a _ _ _ _ _!

Word Tip

outside	stay healthy	spend	be good for
______	______	______	______
햇빛	살이 빠지다	지방을 태우다	활동적인
______	______	______	______

Vocabulary

Connect each picture to the correct meaning.

healthy

ⓐ

① opposite of inside, outdoor

active

ⓑ

② not stay calm, move a lot

outside

ⓒ

③ not sick, very strong health

Writing

Look at the picture below and write your answers.

Hint: Be creative!

(a) What is the boy doing?

→ The boy is r _ _ _ _ _ _ a b _ _ _ _ _ _.

(b) Where is the boy riding a bicycle?

→ He went to the p _ _ _ nearby his h _ _ _ _.

(c) Who is he playing with outside?

→ He is playing outside a _ _ _ _.

The Youngest Everest Climber

On May 22, 2010, a 13-year-old American boy surprised the world. He reached the top of Mt. Everest! The boy's name is Jordan Romero. He became the youngest person to climb the world's highest mountain. Mt. Everest is 8,850 meters high! Now, Jordan is planning to climb the other highest peaks in six other continents. Good luck, Jordan!

Staff reporter Samuel Sohn

Comprehension

Which is not true according to the article?

(a) Mt. Everest is the highest mountain in the world.

(b) A special boy named Jordan Romero reached the top of Mt. Everest.

(c) Aliens attacked Mt. Everest on May 22.

(d) A 13-year-old American boy climbed Mt. Everest on May 22.

Word Tip

surprise ______	reach ______	top ______	the youngest ______
오르다, 등반하다 ______	가장 높은 ______	~할 계획이다 ______	대륙 ______

Grammar

Circle the right word to complete each sentence.

(a) Mt. Everest [**is** / **are** / **isn't**] 8,850 meters high.

(b) A 13-year-old American boy surprised [**the** / **some** / **many**] world.

(c) [**It** / **We** / **He**] became the youngest person to climb the world's highest mountain.

(d) Jordan is planning [**to** / **of** / **for**] climb the other highest peaks.

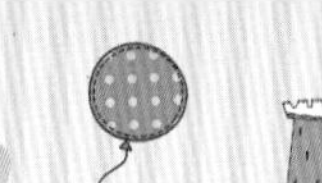

Writing

Look at the picture below. Complete the sentences to answer the questions.

(a) What is this? → It is ________________.

(b) What is it covered with? → It is covered ________________.

(c) Why is it famous? → Because it is the world's ________________.

Vocabulary

Let's think of words that could be used to describe Mt. Everest.

(a) Ama __ __ __ __

(b) Hi __ __

(c) Sn __ __

(d) Co __ __

UNIT 07

The Smallest Monkey in the World

There are about 125 kinds of monkeys in the world. The Baboon is the largest monkey. The Pygmy Marmoset is the smallest monkey in the world. It lives in the tropical rain forests of South America. So, how small is it? It is only 35 centimeters long, including the tail. It weighs about 80-100 grams. It lives in trees for most of its life.

Staff reporter Daniel Chang

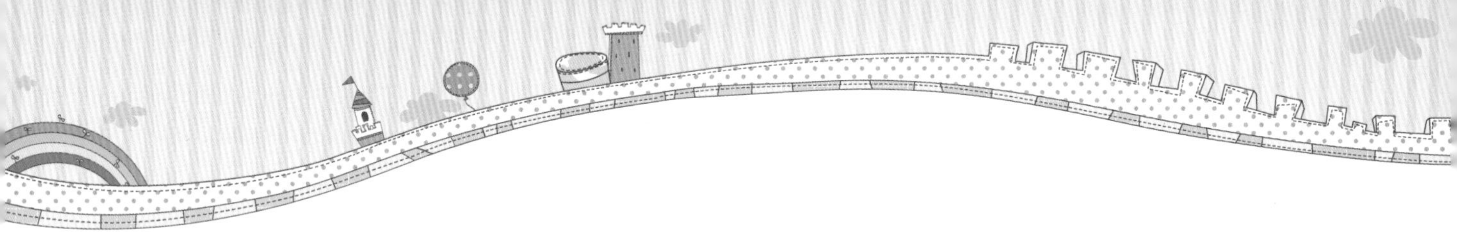

comprehension

Let's look at the picture and fill in the blanks.

Hint: Answers are in the article.

(a) These are the ______________ named Pygmy Marmoset.

(b) They are the ______________ monkeys in the world.

(c) They are only 35 centimeters ____________ including their tails.

(d) They ______________ about 80–100 grams.

(e) They live in ____________________.

Word Tip

kind ____________	the largest ____________	the smallest ____________	live in ____________
tropical ____________	열대 우림 ____________	~을 포함하여 ____________	꼬리 ____________
무게가 ~이다 ____________	대부분 ____________		

02 Question Vocabulary

Connect each picture to the correct meaning.

tropical

ⓐ

① A large area where trees grow close together

forest

ⓑ

② Weather which is very hot and humid near the equator

tail

ⓒ

③ The part extending beyond the end of an animal's body

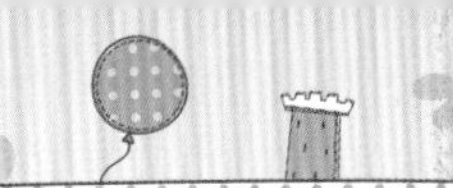

Writing

Look at the picture below and write your own answers.

Hint: Be creative!

(a) Why is the monkey looking downward?

→ He is looking downward searching for some ______________________

____.

(b) Where is the monkey now?

→ He is on the ______________ of a banana tree.

(c) How old does he look? Does he look young or old?

→ He doesn't look so ______________________________________

____.

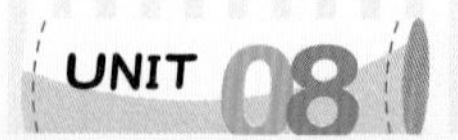

Play Safely in the Playground!

Playing in the playground is a lot of fun. There are many fun things to do. But you have to be careful when playing in the playground. Many children get hurt while playing there. If you find something dangerous, don't touch it and tell your mom or dad right away. Do not push other children either. Always play safely in the playground!

Staff reporter Erica Choi

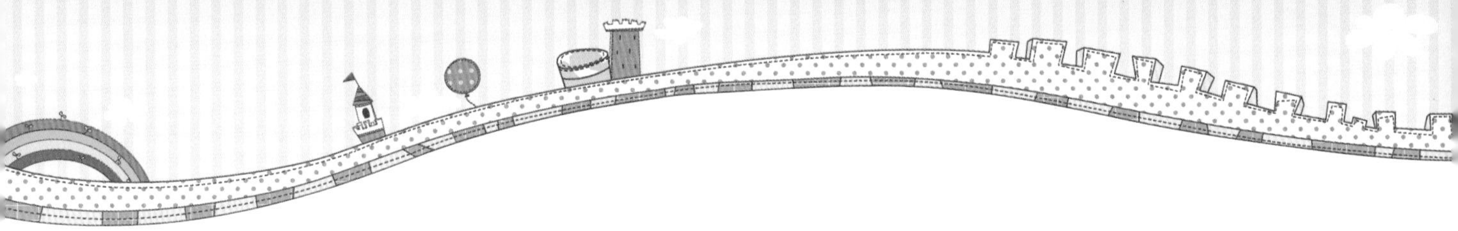

Writing

Complete the sentences by filling in the blanks.

(a) Playing in the **p** _ _ _ _ _ _ _ _ _ is a lot of fun.

(b) But you have to be **c** _ _ _ _ _ _ when playing in the playground.

(c) If you find something **d** _ _ _ _ _ _ _ _, don't touch it and tell your mom or dad right away.

(d) Do not **p** _ _ _ other children. Always play **s** _ _ _ _ _ in the playground!

Word Tip

playground ______	have to ______	be careful ______	get hurt ______
while ~ing ______	dangerous ______	만지다 ______	즉시, 곧바로 ______
밀다 ______	안전하게 ______		

Vocabulary I

Let's complete the crossword puzzle.

Words

DANGEROUS (▼) / HURT (▶) / CAREFUL (▶)
TELL (▶) / PLAYING (▼) / SAFELY (▶) / FIND (▶)

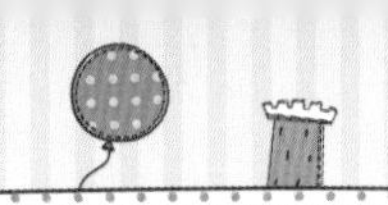

Vocabulary Ⅱ

Let's find the matching words.

push　　be careful　　playground　　dangerous　　get hurt

(a) 위험한 (　　　　　　　　　　)

(b) 놀이터 (　　　　　　　　　　)

(c) 조심하다 (　　　　　　　　　　)

(d) 다치다 (　　　　　　　　　　)

(e) 밀다 (　　　　　　　　　　)

Comprehension

Circle O if the statement is true, and circle X if the statement is false.

(a) Playing in the playground is a lot of fun. **O / X**

(b) You don't have to be careful when playing in the playground. **O / X**

(c) If you find something dangerous, you should not touch it. **O / X**

(d) You should not push other children. **O / X**

UNIT 09

Remembering Kim Dae-joong

On August 12, 2010, a statue of Kim Dae-joong was opened to the public in Jeollanam-do. He served as president from 1998 to 2003. He worked hard for Korea and the world. He received the Nobel Peace Prize in 2000. Mr. Kim passed away on August 18, 2009 at the age of 85. Many people still miss him very much. With his statue, he will be remembered forever!

Staff reporter Daniel Chang

Writing I

Use the words below when you make the sentences.

Nobel Peace Prize / former / President / make
memorize / Kim Dae-joong / statue / Korea

(a) What was this statue made for?

→ This statue ______________________________.

(b) Who was Kim Dae-joong?

→ He was ______________________________.

(c) What kind of prize did he receive in 2000?

→ He received ______________________________.

Word Tip

statue	serve as	work hard for	노벨 평화상
________	________	________	________
~의 나이에	그리워(보고 싶어)하다		
________	________		

Question 02 Grammar

Circle the right word to make the sentence correct.

(a) On August 12, a statue of Kim Dae-joong was [opened / opening / to open] to the public in Jeollanam-do.

(b) He served [to / as / in] president from 1998 to 2003. He worked hard [on / for / to] Korea and the world.

(c) He received the Nobel Peace Prize [into / in / during] 2000.

(d) Mr. Kim passed [in / away / out] on August 18, 2009 at the age of 85.

Question 03 Writing II

Write your own story describing the picture below.

Hint: Be creative!

Who is he?

____

____

____

____

____

____

____

____

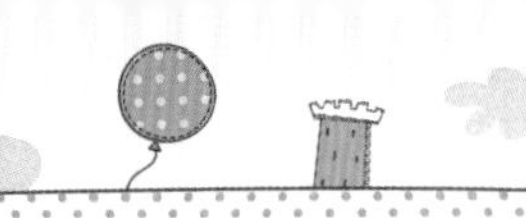
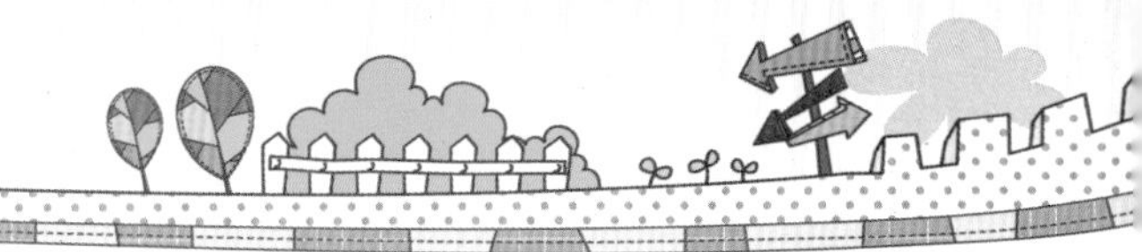

Vocabulary

Let's finish the cross word puzzle below related to the story.

Across

① It's similar with the word "memorize."

② Large sculpture of animal or person made of stone or metal

Down

③ It's similar with the word "yet."

④ It's similar with the word "harmony" and the antonym is "war."

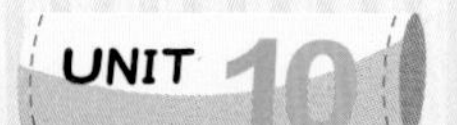

I Have the Longest Mustache in America!

In America, many men grow mustaches. A mustache is hair, which a man grows above his upper lip. A gentleman named Larry McClure has the longest mustache in America. He lives in San Francisco. His mustache is nearly 80 centimeters long! Larry is very proud of his mustache. He spends 45 minutes every day washing and drying it!

Staff reporter Daniel Chang

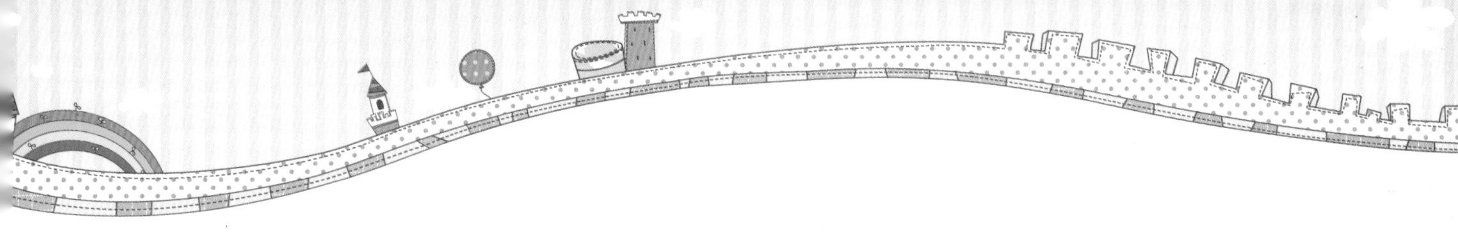

01 Question Writing

Fill in the blanks with the right words.

grow / mustache / upper / lip
America / proud / minutes / drying

(a) A gentleman from America has a very long ______________________.

(b) He is very ______________________ of his 80-centimeter-long mustache.

(c) He spends 45 ____________________ every day washing and drying his mustache.

Word Tip

grow	mustache	upper lip	nearly
길이가 ~인	~을 아주 자랑스럽게 여기다	(시간을) 보내다	

Comprehension

Look at the sentences below and decide whether they are true (o) or false (x).

(a) A mustache is hair, where a man grows above his head. **O / X**

(b) Larry McClure lives in San Francisco, a city in America. **O / X**

(c) Larry feels very ashamed of his mustache but he doesn't have the money to cut it. **O / X**

Vocabulary I

Choose the right word to complete each sentence.

(a) A mustache is hair, where a man grows above his [**shoulder** / **upper lip** / **knee**].

(b) His mustache is nearly 80 centimeters [**long** / **short** / **thin**].

(c) He spends 45 minutes every day [**washing** / **watching** / **wishing**] and drying his mustache.

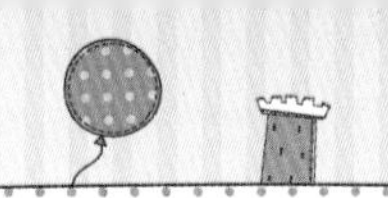

Vocabulary II

Let's find the words from the story in this word puzzle!

A	W	E	V	E	R	Y	N	H	I
G	C	Q	E	P	O	Q	D	D	U
B	N	M	G	A	R	F	G	E	O
E	S	U	D	S	E	O	F	G	P
G	R	S	B	R	K	D	U	R	K
H	F	T	J	H	R	U	H	D	R
Y	H	A	I	R	F	B	N	P	O
K	B	C	Y	I	L	W	O	R	G
L	J	H	T	O	P	A	B	S	Z
K	Y	E	N	J	H	G	F	E	C

Words

GROW / HAIR / MUSTACHE
PROUD / EVERY

UNIT 11

The Most Popular Soccer Player in the World

Who is your favorite soccer player? On May 7, 2010, British magazine OK chose David Beckham as the most popular soccer player in the world. He is a great player. He is also famous for his good looks and fashion sense. The 36-year-old player is loved by many soccer fans all over the world. Sadly, he couldn't play in the 2010 World Cup because he hurt his legs. Don't get hurt any more, David!

Staff reporter Samuel Sohn

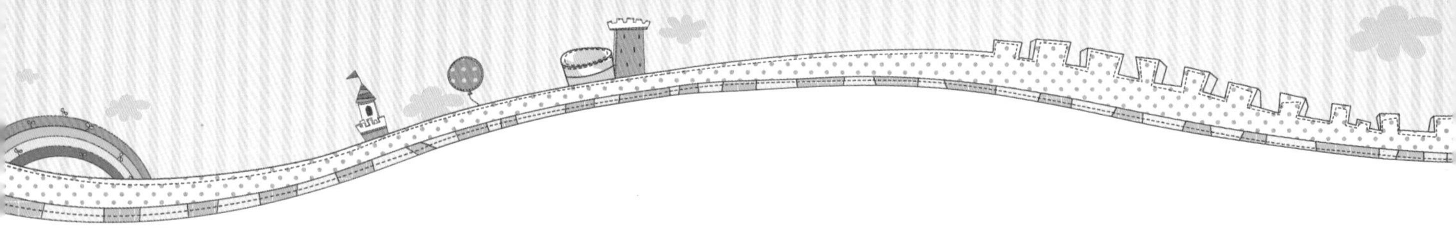

Writing

Let's look at the picture. Fill in the blanks and complete the sentences.

① number ② soccer ③ wearing ④ handsome ⑤ holding

(a) David Beckham is ( ) his thumbs up.

(b) He is ( ) his uniform.

(c) His ( ) is seven.

(d) He is an English ( ) player.

(e) He is a ( ) guy.

Word Tip

favorite ________	British ________	magazine ________	chose ________
famous for ________	외모 ________	패션 감각 ________	다치다, 부상당하다 ________
세계 도처에 ________			

02 Question Grammar

Circle the right word to complete each sentence.

(a) [**Who** / **Whom** / **Whose**] is your favorite soccer player?

(b) David Beckham is the [**more** / **most** / **good**] popular soccer player in the world.

(c) David is famous [**of** / **from** / **for**] his good looks and fashion sense.

(d) The [**36-year-old** / **36-years-old** / **36-years-olds**] player is loved by many soccer fans all over the world.

(e) David couldn't play in the 2010 World Cup [**although** / **because** / **while**] he hurt his legs.

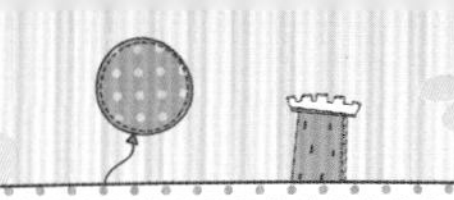
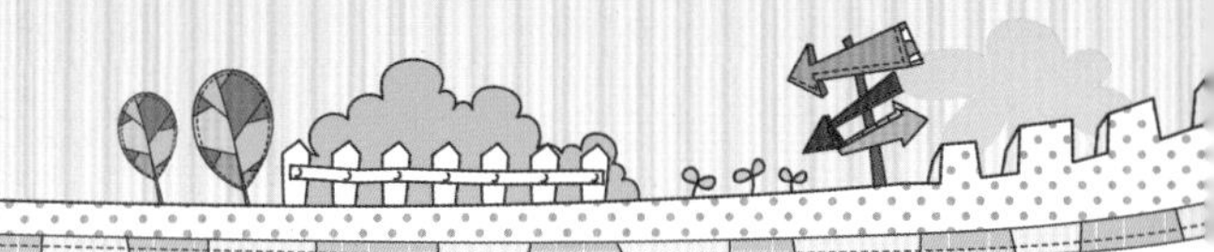

Vocabulary

Find the words used in the story in the puzzle below.

L	O	W	S	W	W	E	I	Y	P
H	L	C	Z	L	S	I	P	G	O
B	F	A	V	O	R	I	T	E	P
L	E	C	C	G	R	H	H	U	U
Z	S	C	S	U	O	M	A	F	L
H	E	J	K	Y	D	I	L	B	A
R	Z	U	L	H	F	D	L	F	R
A	V	J	X	Y	A	L	S	G	V
B	C	W	B	R	X	M	W	E	E
A	V	O	H	W	W	X	W	M	D

Words

BECKHAM / FAMOUS / FAVORITE
POPULAR / SOCCER

How Do I Look in the Portrait?

Can you guess who the woman in the picture is? She is the American First Lady. Yes, her name is Michelle Obama! On August 20, 2010, her portrait was opened to the public at the National Portrait Gallery in Washington D.C. The gallery chose her as one of the most famous Americans. Mrs. Obama's portrait was on view for one year.

Staff reporter Erica Choi

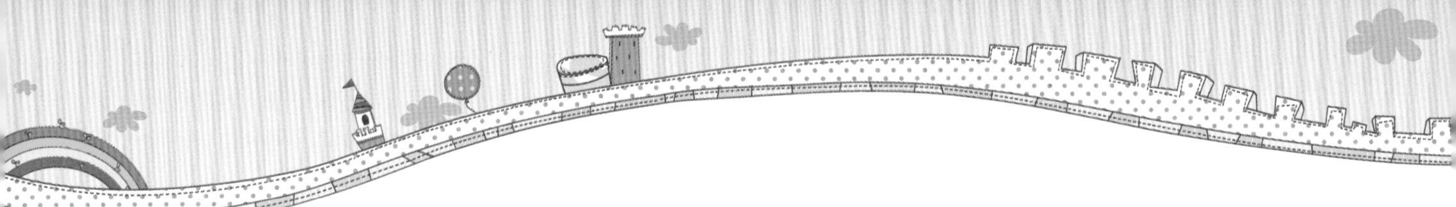

Comprehension I

Read each question and find the right answer.

(a) What is the main topic of the article?

① The dress of Michelle Obama
② The dish of Michelle Obama
③ The portrait of Michelle Obama
④ The contribution of Michelle Obama

(b) Write down three words that begin with "P" in the article.

① ____________________

② ____________________

③ ____________________

(c) How long was the Michelle Obama's portrait on view?

For _ _ _ _ _ _ _

Word Tip

guess ____________	portrait ____________	be opened to the public ____________	갤러리, 전시실 ____________
A를 B로 선정하다 ____________	전시되다 ____________		

Vocabulary

Choose the right word to complete each sentence.

(a) Michelle Obama is the American ___________.

① First Lady
② President
③ Prime Minister
④ Artist

(b) The portrait was opened to the ________ at the National Portrait Gallery.

① picture
② person
③ public
④ poem

(c) The gallery chose her as _________ the most famous Americans.

① some
② two of
③ one of
④ any

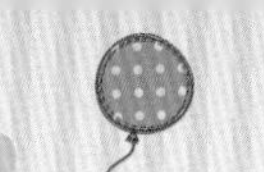

Comprehension Ⅱ

Look at the picture below and then answer the questions about it.

(a) What is this?

① The portrait of the American First Lady.
② The photo of the American First Lady.
③ The portrait of the Korean First Lady.
④ The photo of the Korean First Lady.

(b) What does "First Lady" mean?

① The sister of the President.
② The wife of the President.
③ The biggest woman in the country.
④ The richest woman in the country.

(c) Choose the word that explains "The event being on view."

① exhibition　　② explore
③ excitement　　④ explain

UNIT 13

Do Zebras Lie Down When They Sleep?

Zebras are interesting animals. They look like horses. But they have black and white stripes on their bodies. Their stripes look similar, but each zebra has unique stripe pattern! These plant-eating animals live in large groups. So, do they lie down to sleep at night? No! Zebras sleep while they are standing up! How interesting!

Staff reporter Daniel Chang

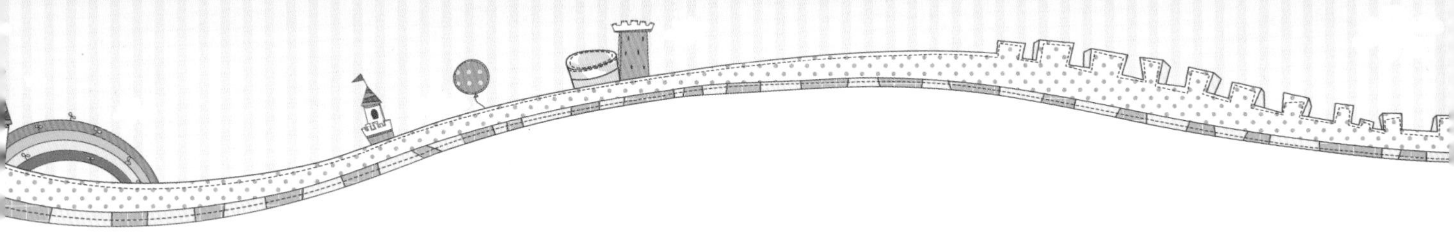

Comprehension

Let's look at the picture and fill in the blanks.

Hint: Answers are in the article.

(a) There are many z __ __ __ __ __ in the picture.

(b) Each zebra has a unique st __ __ __ __ pattern.

(c) Their stripes look s __ __ __ __ __ __.

(d) They don't __ __ e down to sleep.

(e) They are pl __ __ __ - eating animals.

Word Tip

zebra	look like	stripe	similar
unique	무늬, 모양	식물을 먹는	눕다
밤에	서다		

Vocabulary

Connect each picture to the correct meaning.

Unique

ⓐ ① When the sun falls

Sleep

ⓑ ② Snoring and having dreams

Night

ⓒ ③ Very different

Writing

Look at the picture below and write your answers.

Hint: Be creative!

(a) What do you think the zebras are doing?

→ They are running to go **som** __ __ __ __ __ __.

(b) Where are the zebras now?

→ They are probably running on the field of **Afr** __ __ __.

(c) Don't the zebras look serious? Are they mad?

→ No, the zebras don't look so **ser** __ __ __ __ or **m** __ __.

UNIT 14

Walking Safety

Walking is a wonderful exercise. It is good for your health. It helps you maintain a healthy weight, too. But you have to remember a few things for your safety; never walk alone. Always walk with your mom or dad. When walking down busy streets, hold their hands. Also, watch out for cars and stay away from the edge of the sidewalk. Keep to these simple rules and enjoy walking!

Staff reporter Daniel Chang

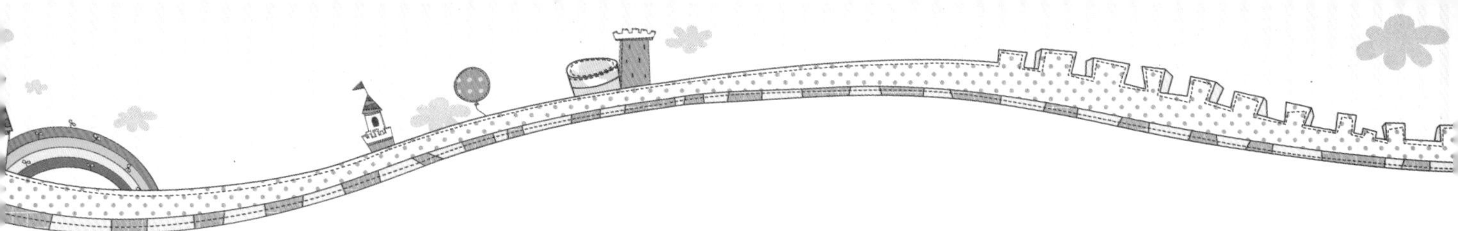

01 Question Comprehension

Let's look at the picture and fill in the blanks.

Hint: Answers are in the article.

(a) Walking is a wonderful e __ __ __ __ __ __ __.

(b) It helps you m __ __ __ __ __ __ __ a healthy w __ __ __ __ __.

(c) You have to remember a few things for your s __ __ __ __ __
; never walk a __ __ __ __.

(d) Watch out for cars and stay a __ __ __ from the edge of the s __ __ __ __ __ __ __.

Word Tip

exercise	maintain	weight	remember
a few	safety	never	alone
길을 걷다	손을 잡다	조심하다	~에서 떨어져 있다
가장자리	보도, 인도		

Vocabulary

Connect each picture to the correct meaning.

watch out

ⓐ

① to be careful

sidewalk

ⓑ

② to keep something in your hand or to grab something

hold

ⓒ

③ a paved path made for people to walk safely on

Writing

Look at the picture below and write your answers.

Hint: walk, family, shirt, skirt, meet

(a) What is the girl doing?

→ She is ____________________ on a beach.

(b) What is she wearing?

→ She is wearing ____.

(c) Where is she going?

→ She is going to ____.

UNIT 15

Take Care of Your Ears!

Your ears are very important. You need to take good care of your ears. To protect your ears, do not listen to music loudly using earphones or headphones. Also, do not fall asleep with earphones in. After taking a shower, don't pick your ears with cotton swabs. Lastly, before going out, make sure to put sun block on your ears; They are very sensitive to the sun!

Staff reporter Daniel Chang

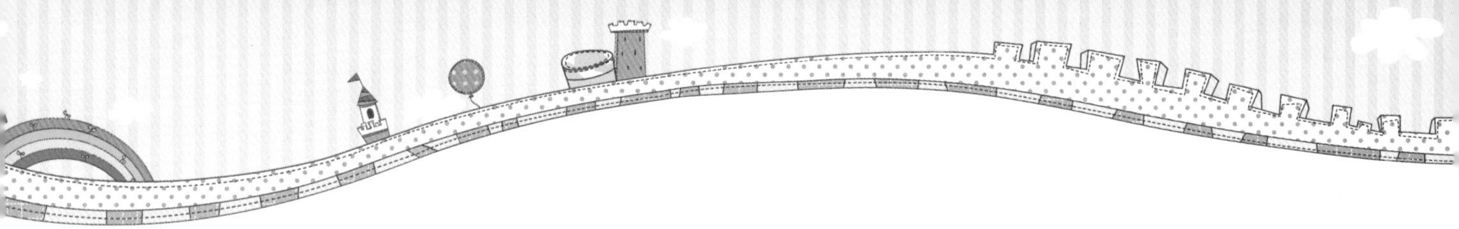

01 Question

Comprehension

Let's look at the picture and fill in the blanks.

Hint: Answers are in the article.

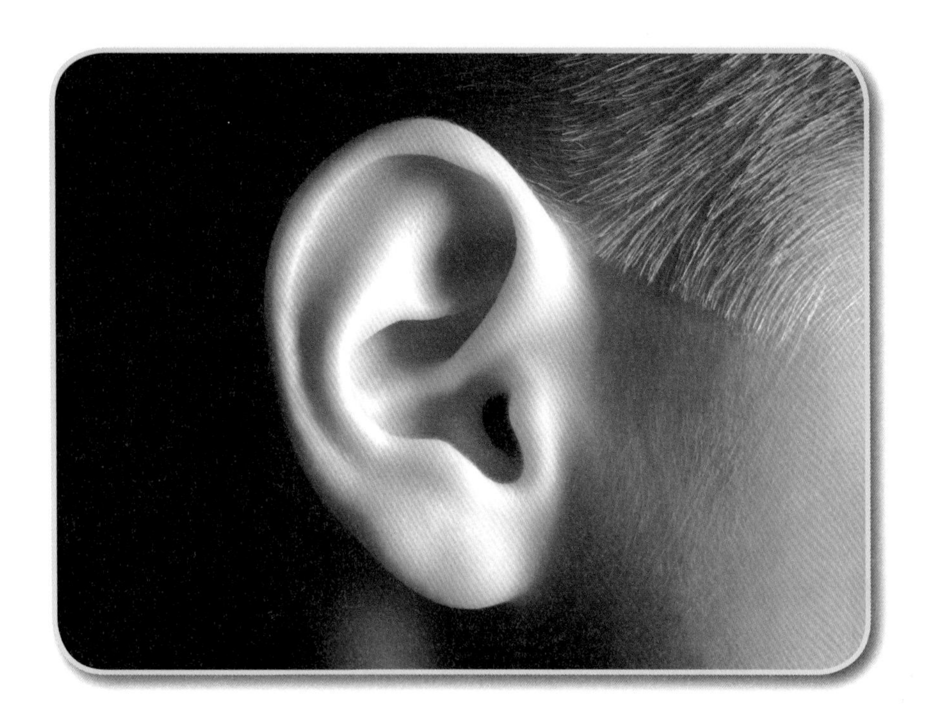

(a) Your ears are very i _ _ _ _ _ _ _ _.

(b) You need to take g _ _ _   c _ _ _ of your ears.

(c) Also, do not f _ _ _   a _ _ _ _ _ with earphones in.

(d) After taking a s _ _ _ _ _, don't p_ _ _ your ears with cotton swabs.

Word Tip

important	take good care of	protect	listen to
loudly	fall asleep	샤워를 하다	면봉
마지막으로	외출하다, 밖에 나가다	~을 확실히 하다	민감한

Vocabulary

Connect each picture to the correct meaning.

protect

ⓐ

① cream people put to avoid the sunburn

sun block

ⓑ

② to keep something from being damaged or injured

sensitive

ⓒ

③ easily response to other things

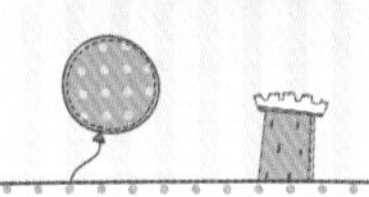

Writing

Look at the picture below and write your answers.

Hint: Be creative!

(a) What are you listening to?

→ I am listening to my **f** _ _ _ _ _ _ _ song.

(b) When do you listen to music?

→ I **l** _ _ _ _ _ to music before I go to **b** _ _.

(c) What musical instruments do you like to play?

→ I like **p** _ _ _ _ _ _ the **p** _ _ _ _ and the **v** _ _ _ _ _.

ANSWERS

UNIT 01

Word Tip

종류 / 가장 작은 / 힌트 / 무게가 나가다 / 아주 작은 / ~에 살다 / (날개를) 퍼덕거리다 / wing / time / per second / backwards / guess / Bee Hummingbird

1. Writing
(a) ③
(b) ①
(c) ⑤
(d) ④
(e) ②

2. Grammar
(a) seen
(b) many
(c) times
(d) fly
(e) of

3. Vocabulary

M	A	G	L	W	S	W	B	R	O
G	D	O	Q	A	V	H	I	N	T
W	J	G	B	S	G	G	R	C	E
L	E	G	C	H	E	M	D	S	T
H	T	I	N	Y	U	E	L	T	M
J	V	Y	G	E	F	R	F	A	N
S	T	Y	K	H	H	G	I	R	W
P	O	A	C	R	L	W	Q	I	E
P	B	A	O	W	Y	H	N	I	B
Q	E	X	P	E	N	G	I	V	E

UNIT 02

Word Tip

기념하다, 축하하다 / 태어나다 / 대통령 / leader / respect / stay healthy

1. Writing I
(a) Nelson Mandela, the former President of South Africa.
(b) celebrating Nelson Mandela's 93rd birthday.
(c) still respect him.

2. Grammar
(a) On
(b) was born
(c) from
(d) still

3. Writing II
Today is my grandma's 101st birthday. She is blowing the candles on the cake. The cake in front of her is decorated with beautiful flowers. She is celebrating her birthday with her family and friends.

4. Vocabulary

UNIT 03

Word Tip

~이 되다 / 여성 / 지도자 / 약속하다 / work hard for / work as / better

1. Comprehension
(a) ②
(b) first / female / from
(c) January 1, 2011

2. Vocabulary
(a) ③
(b) ④
(c) ①

3. Comprehension
(a) ④
(b) ②
(c) ③

UNIT 04

Word Tip

가장 긴 / 혀 / according to / live in / be surprised

1. Writing
(a) ②
(b) ④
(c) ①
(d) ⑤
(e) ③

2. Grammar
(a) at
(b) Who
(c) to
(d) has
(e) long

3. Vocabulary

M	A	G	L	Z	X	W	D	R	O
G	D	O	Q	D	C	E	A	V	I
B	N	O	T	Y	G	C	F	C	E
G	J	G	F	E	F	U	P	S	M
C	T	O	N	G	U	E	I	K	A
V	V	Y	U	E	F	R	F	J	N
O	I	C	K	I	P	O	W	Z	A
I	U	A	C	R	L	W	Q	H	E
P	R	A	U	I	P	Y	T	G	F
Q	X	S	T	B	W	O	R	L	D

UNIT 05

Word Tip

밖에서 / 건강을 유지하다 / (시간을) 쓰다 / ~에 좋다 / daylight / lose weight / burn fat / active

1. Comprehension
(a) healthy, spend

(b) weight
(c) burn
(d) active

2. Vocabulary
ⓐ – ③
ⓑ – ②
ⓒ – ①

3.Writing
(a) riding, bicycle
(b) park, house
(c) alone

UNIT 

Word Tip
놀라게 하다 / 도달하다 / 정상, 꼭대기 / 가장 어린 / climb / the highest / plan to / continent

1. Comprehension
(c)

2. Grammar
(a) is
(b) the
(c) He
(d) to

3. Writing
(a) Mt. Everest
(b) with snow
(c) highest mountain

4. Vocabulary
(a) Amazing
(b) High
(c) Snow
(d) Cold

UNIT 

Word Tip
종류 / 가장 큰 / 가장 작은 / ~에 살다 / 열대의 / tropical rain forest / including / tail / weigh / most

1. Comprehension
(a) monkeys
(b) smallest
(c) long
(d) weigh
(e) trees

2. Vocabulary
ⓐ – ②
ⓑ – ①
ⓒ – ③

3. Writing
(a) insects for his dinner
(b) leaf
(c) old. He looks young to me because he is so small.

UNIT 

Word Tip
놀이터, 운동장 / ~해야만 한다 / 조심하다 / 다치다 / ~하는 동안 / 위험한 / touch / right away / push / safely

1. Writing
(a) playground
(b) careful
(c) dangerous
(d) push, safely

2. Vocabulary I

3. Vocabulary II
(a) dangerous
(b) playground
(c) be careful
(d) get hurt
(e) push

4. Comprehension
(a) O
(b) X
(c) O
(d) O

UNIT 

Word Tip
동상 / ~의 역할을 하다 / ~을 위해 열심히 일하다 / Nobel peace prize / at the age of / miss

1. Writing I
(a) was made for memorizing Kim Dae-joong
(b) the former president of Korea
(c) the Nobel Peace Prize in 2000

2. Grammar
(a) opened
(b) as, for
(c) in
(d) away

3. Writing II
He is Kim Dae-joong, the former president of Korea. He passed away in 2009, but a lot of people still remember him. He was very warm-hearted person who acted an important role between South and North Koreas. Though he passed away, Korean people still remember him.

4. Vocabulary

UNIT 10

Word Tip

기르다 / 콧수염 / 윗입술 / 거의 / long / be very proud of / spend

1. Writing
(a) mustache
(b) proud
(c) minutes

2. Comprehension
(a) X
(b) O
(c) X

3. Vocabulary I
(a) upper lip
(b) long
(c) washing

4. Vocabulary II

A	W	E	V	E	R	Y	N	H	I
G	C	Q	E	P	O	Q	D	D	U
B	N	M	G	A	R	F	G	E	O
E	S	U	D	S	E	O	F	G	P
G	R	S	B	R	K	D	U	R	K
H	F	T	J	H	R	U	H	D	R
Y	H	A	I	R	F	B	N	P	O
K	B	C	Y	I	L	W	O	R	G
L	J	H	T	O	P	A	B	S	Z
K	Y	E	N	J	H	G	F	E	C

UNIT 11

Word Tip

매우 좋아하는 / 영국의 / 잡지 / 선택했다 / ~로 유명한 / look / fashion sense / get hurt / all over the world

1. Writing
(a) ⑤
(b) ③
(c) ①
(d) ②
(e) ④

2. Grammar
(a) Who
(b) most
(c) for
(d) 35-year-old
(e) because

3. Vocabulary

L	O	W	S	W	W	E	I	Y	P
H	L	C	Z	L	S	I	P	G	O
B	F	A	V	O	R	I	T	E	P
L	E	C	C	G	R	H	H	U	U
Z	S	C	S	U	O	M	A	F	L
H	E	J	K	Y	D	I	L	B	A
R	Z	U	L	H	F	D	L	F	R
A	V	J	X	Y	A	L	S	G	V
B	C	W	B	R	X	M	W	E	E
A	V	O	H	W	W	X	W	M	D

UNIT 12

Word Tip

짐작하다, 추측하다 / 초상화 / 대중에게 개방되다 / gallery / choose A as B / be on view

1. Comprehension I
(a) ③
(b) picture / portrait / public
(c) one year

2. Vocabulary
(a) ①
(b) ③
(c) ③

3. Comprehension II
(a) ①
(b) ②
(c) ①

UNIT 13

Word Tip

얼룩말 / ~처럼 보이다 / 줄무늬 / 비슷한 / 독특한 / pattern / plant-eating / lie (down) / at night / stand up

1. Comprehension
(a) zebras
(b) stripe
(c) similar
(d) lie
(e) plant

2. Vocabulary
ⓐ – ③
ⓑ – ②
ⓒ – ①

3. Writing
(a) somewhere
(b) Africa
(c) serious or mad

UNIT 14

Word Tip

운동 / 유지하다 / 몸무게 / 기억하다 / 조금 / 안전 / 결코~않다 / 혼자서 / walk down streets / hold hands / watch out / stay away from / edge / sidewalk

1. Comprehension
(a) exercise

(b) maintain, weight
(c) safety, alone
(d) away, sidewalk

2. Vocabulary

ⓐ – ①
ⓑ – ③
ⓒ – ②

3. Writing

(a) walking
(b) a pink shirt and a blue skirt
(c) meet her family

Word Tip

중요한 / 잘 보살피다 / 보호하다 / 듣다 / 크게 / 잠들다 / take a shower / cotton swab / lastly / go out / make sure (to) / sensitive

1. Comprehension

(a) important
(b) good care
(c) fall asleep
(d) shower, pick

2. Vocabulary

ⓐ – ②
ⓑ – ①
ⓒ – ③

3. Writing

(a) favorite
(b) listen, bed
(c) playing, piano, violin

MEMO

MEMO

MEMO